Who Ate It?

A Book about Pronouns

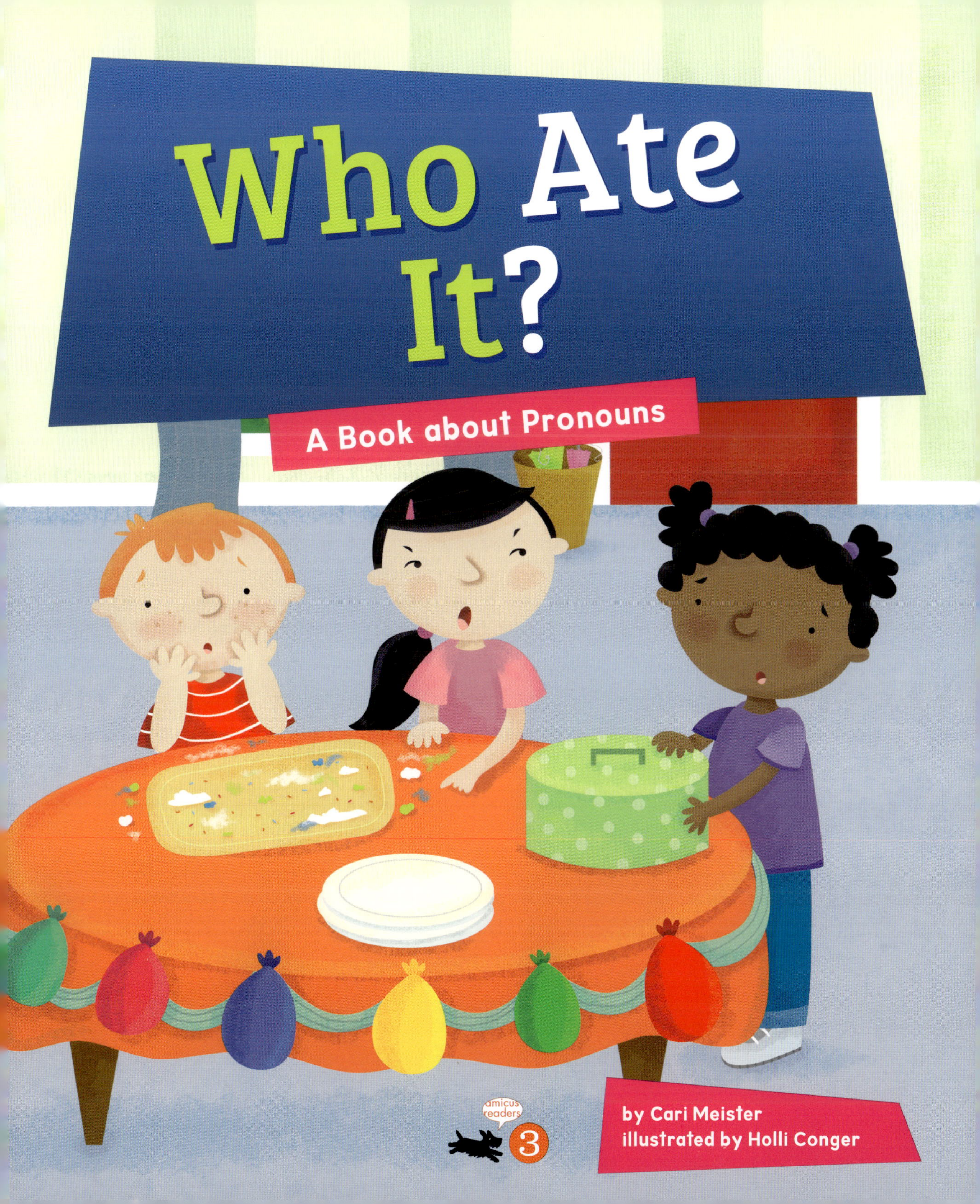

by Cari Meister
illustrated by Holli Conger

amicus readers

Say Hello to Amicus Readers.

You'll find our helpful dog, Amicus, chasing a ball—to let you know the reading level of a book.

1

Learn to Read

High frequency words and close photo-text matches introduce familiar topics and provide support for brand new readers.

2

Read Independently

Some repetition is mixed with varied sentence structures and a select amount of new vocabulary words are introduced with text and photo support.

3

Read to Know More

Interesting facts and engaging art and photos give fluent readers fun books both for reading practice and to learn about new topics.

Amicus Readers are published by Amicus
P.O. Box 1329, Mankato, MN 56002
www.amicuspublishing.us

Illustrations by Holli Conger
Editor Wendy Dieker
Designer Heather Dreisbach

Printed in the United States of America.

10 9 8 7 6 5 4 3 2 1

Library of Congress Cataloging-in-Publication Data
Names: Meister, Cari, author. | Conger, Holli, illustrator.
Title: Who ate it? : a book about pronouns / by Cari Meister ; illustrated by Holli Conger.
Description: Mankato, Minnesota : Amicus, [2016] | Series: Say What? Parts of Speech| Audience: K to Grade 3._
Identifiers: LCCN 2015041477 (print) | LCCN 2015048391 (ebook) | ISBN 9781607539377 (library binding) | ISBN 9781681510613 (eBook)
Subjects: LCSH: English language--Pronoun--Juvenile literature. | English language--Parts of speech--Juvenile literature. | English language--Grammar--Juvenile literature. | Language arts (Elementary)
Classification: LCC PE1261 .M45 2016 (print) | LCC PE1261 (ebook) | DDC 428.2--dc23
LC record available at http://lccn.loc.gov/2015041477

A pronoun is a word that takes place of a noun. A noun is a person, place, or thing. The **purple** words in the story are pronouns.

William and Ping are making a cake. **They** bake **it**. **They** frost **it**.

Bernard's birthday is today. William and Ping want to surprise him.

William says, "Look! Scarlett and Arjun are here."

Ping says, "Let's go outside with them. We can play until Bernard gets here!"

A little while later, the friends go back inside.

The plate is there. But the cake is gone!

"Someone ate it!" says William.

"Did you eat it?" Ping asks Scarlett.

"Eat what?" asks Scarlett.

"The cake we made for Bernard."

"Me?" asks Scarlett. "I don't even like cake."

"Maybe your little sister ate it," says Ping.

William says, "My sister didn't eat it. She is too little."

"Did you eat it?" Scarlett asks Arjun.

"No," he says. "I just got here."

"Who ate it?" asks William.

Just then, Baxter trots in. He has frosting all over his face.

“Oh no!” says William. “Baxter ate the cake!”

Happy
Birthday
Bernard!
BAXTER

"Don't worry," says Arjun. "We made Bernard a cake, too!"

"Everybody find your places!" says Scarlett. "I see Bernard coming!"

"Surprise! Happy birthday, Bernard!"

Jobs of a Pronoun

Pronouns can stand for people or things in a sentence.

William and Ping make a cake. They bake it.

They stands for *William and Ping*. It stands for *cake*.

Pronouns can say who something belongs to.

Baxter has frosting all over his face.

Pronouns can take the place of people we don't know.

Someone ate the cake!